PRECIPITATION

water wise

Gail Parman

PowerKiDS press

Published in 2027 by
The Rosen Publishing Group, Inc.
2544 Clinton Street, Buffalo, NY 14224

Designer: Beeline Media and Design
Editor: Tricia Hoffman

Portions of this work were originally authored by Caitie McAneney and published as *Where's the Water?: Precipitation*. All new material in this edition is authored by Gail Parman.

Photo credits: Cover, p. 1 Stone36/Shutterstock.com; Cover, p. 1 SaltyArts Design/Shutterstock.com; cover, p. 1, 4, 6, 8, 10, 12, 14, 16, 18, 20, 21, 24 (wave) vectorstuff/Shutterstock.com; p. 5 Platon Anton/Shutterstock.com; p. 6 Ammak/Shutterstock.com; p. 7 FarisFitrianto/Shutterstock.com; p. 9 gui jun peng/Shutterstock.com; p. 10 Olya Detry/Shutterstock.com; p. 11 MyraMyra/Shutterstock.com; p. 12 AP Tolang/Shutterstock.com; p. 13 Brian Nolan/Shutterstock.com; p. 15 New Africa/Shutterstock.com; p. 17 Jack Parinussa/Shutterstock.com; p. 18 NOAA; p. 19 CherylRamalho/Shutterstock.com; p. 20 kapichka/Shutterstock.com; p. 21 Virdauso/Shutterstock.com

Cataloging-in-Publication Data
Names: Parman, Gail.
Title: Precipitation / Gail Parman.
Description: Buffalo, New York : PowerKids Press, 2027. | Series: Water wise | Includes glossary and index.
Identifiers: ISBN 9781499458312 (pbk.) | ISBN 9781499458329 (library bound) | ISBN 9781499458336 (ebook)
Subjects: LCSH: Precipitation (Meteorology)--Juvenile literature.
Classification: LCC QC920.P377 2027 | DDC 551.577--dc23

Printed in China

CPSIA Compliance Information: Batch #QSPK27. For Further Information contact Rosen Publishing at 1-800-237-9932.

Contents

Don't Get Wet!

You're playing outside when you notice a big, gray cloud in the sky. Uh oh! It's just a matter of time before the precipitation starts. Better get inside!

Water exists on Earth in oceans, lakes, streams, and groundwater. Some water evaporates, or turns into a gas called vapor, and rises into the sky. When this vapor cools down, it changes back into water and falls as rain, snow, or other precipitation. Precipitation could mess up your outdoor playtime, but it is very important for life on Earth!

Go with the Flow

Precipitation is water that falls from the sky. Most precipitation happens as rain or snow. It's an important part of the **water cycle**.

In the water cycle, water moves from Earth's surface, into the **atmosphere**, and returns to Earth. The water cycle affects weather patterns in our world.

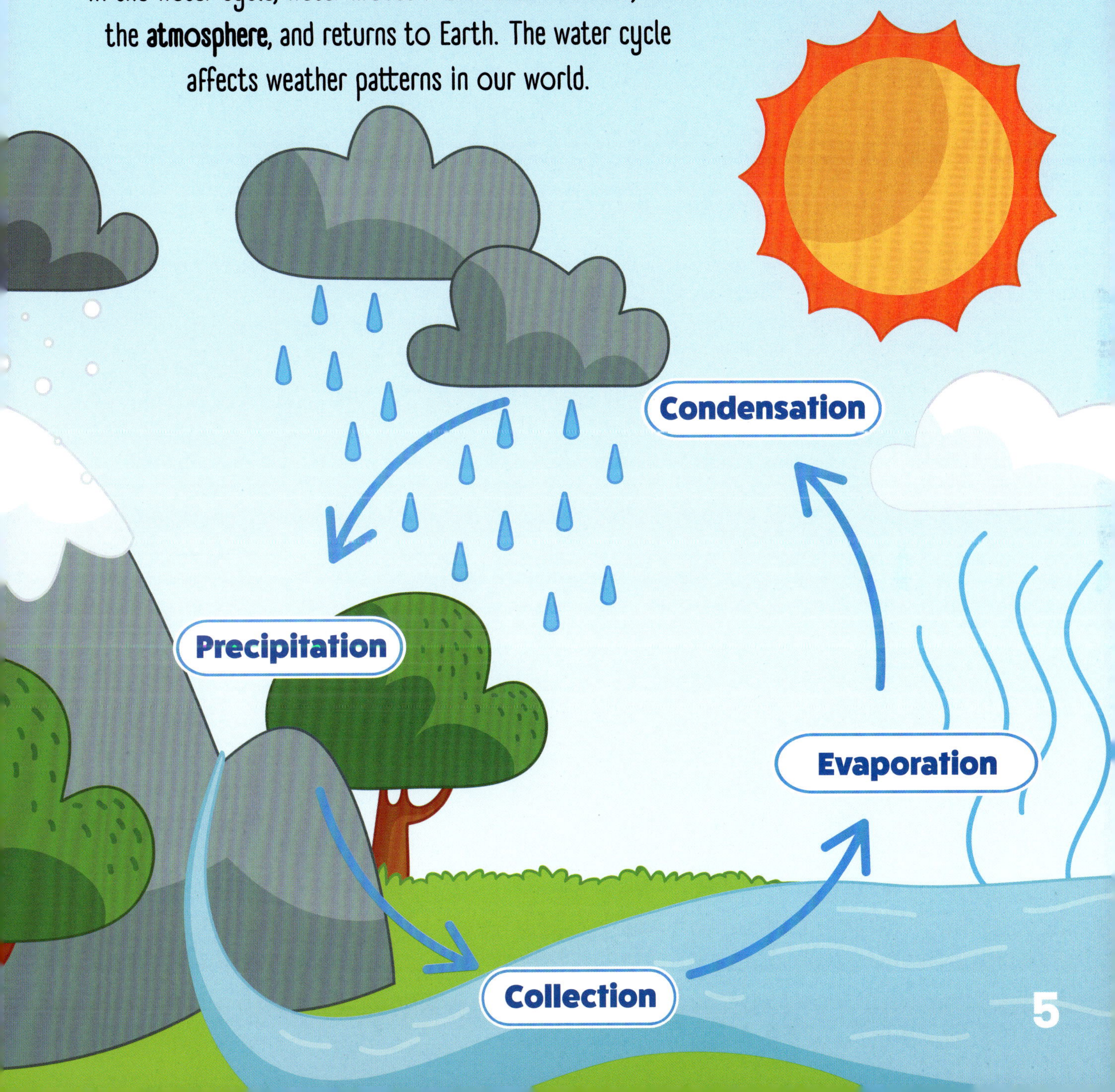

We Need Water

If there was no precipitation on Earth, we wouldn't be able to live here! All living things need some amount of water in order to live and grow.

Plants need rain to make their food. People and animals need to eat plants and drink water. The whole **food chain** depends on water. Many living things live in **temperate** and **tropical** areas that get a lot of rain, such as rainforests. Some places, like deserts, get little precipitation. Fewer living things can survive in such an **extreme** environment.

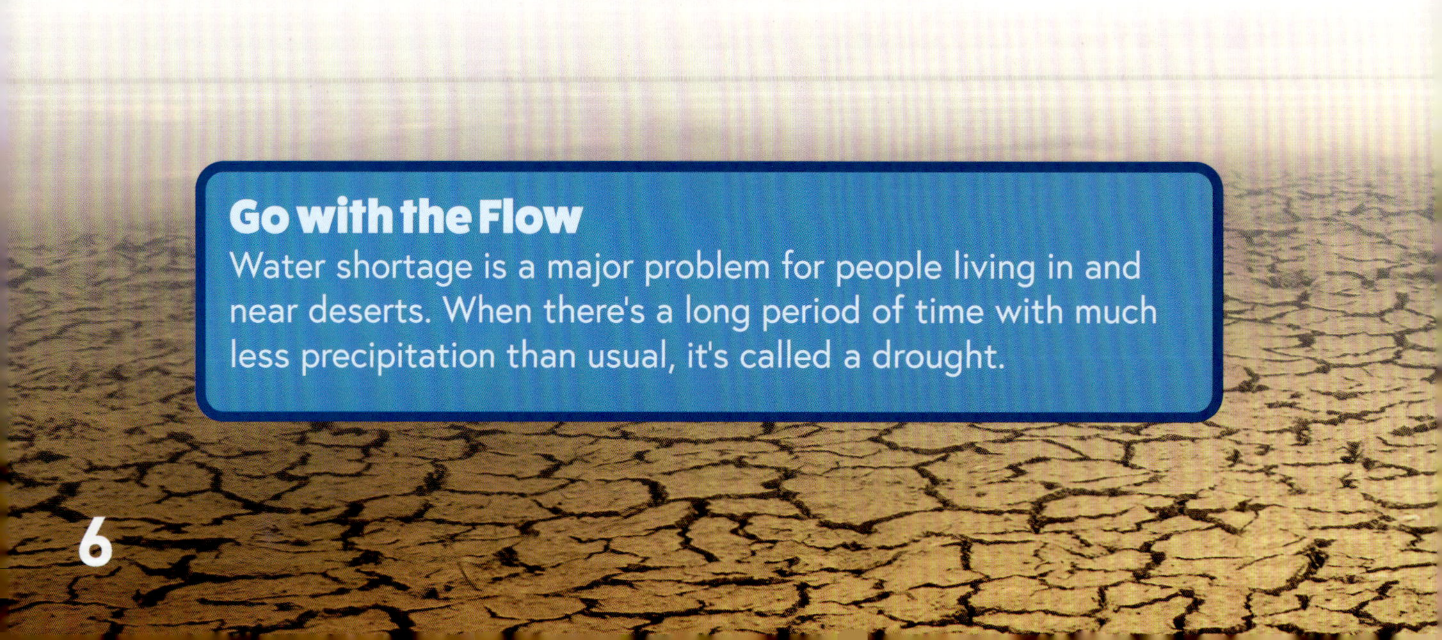

Go with the Flow

Water shortage is a major problem for people living in and near deserts. When there's a long period of time with much less precipitation than usual, it's called a drought.

Groundwater is the underground water that people use for wells, watering crops, and more. Without precipitation, there would be no groundwater for us to use.

Humidity and Fog

Water is everywhere on Earth—even in the air around us! Humidity is the amount of water vapor in the air. The more humid it is, the more water vapor is in the air. Some places, like rainforests, are very humid.

When water vapor comes together, it forms fog if it's near the ground or a cloud if it's high in the sky. Fog and clouds are filled with tiny drops of water called droplets. Sometimes droplets come together and form heavier drops. When they're heavy enough, the drops fall to Earth as rain or snow, depending on the temperature.

Go with the Flow

Have you ever felt sticky or sweaty on a warm day, even if it's not very hot? That's because of humidity! On a humid day, sweat doesn't evaporate as easily, so our bodies feel hotter.

Fog is just a cloud that's near the ground.
The air is thick with water vapor.

Different Types of Rain

Rain happens when water vapor condenses into liquid drops heavy enough to fall. But not all rain is the same.

When it drizzles, tiny droplets of rain fall from the sky. You might barely feel them at all. Other times, the drops are larger. You might get really wet! This is called a rain shower. Rain showers can last just a few minutes, or they could last all day. If it's cold enough, rain could even fall as sleet. Sleet is a mix of rain and snow that falls as small, wet pellets.

Go with the Flow

Some people collect rainwater in a barrel. This water can be reused to water your garden during dry spells!

Most people would probably rather have a sunny day than a rainy day. But we need rain too!

Extreme Rain

Sometimes, too much rain can be a bad thing. Heavy rain can cause flooding, harm buildings and crops, and even kill people. This type of extreme weather often happens as part of a **hurricane**. In just one day, a hurricane can drop trillions of gallons of rain, which is made even worse by high winds.

Each summer in Southeast Asia, there's extreme rain brought on by a **monsoon**. The heavy rainfall floods towns and cities and can cause dangerous mudslides.

Go with the Flow

Though they can be dangerous, people in Southeast Asia need the summer monsoon rains to water their crops. They also use the rushing water to produce electricity.

In August 2005, Hurricane Katrina was one of the worst hurricanes ever to hit the United States. Millions of people lost their homes and more than 1,800 people died. Some areas of Louisiana stayed flooded for weeks afterward.

Sleet and Hail

When the temperature is warm, precipitation falls as rain. When it's cold, precipitation falls as snow. But what happens when the temperature is somewhere in the middle?

Sleet happens when snow melts as it falls and then freezes again before reaching the ground. This type of precipitation is more like icy slush than fluffy snow.

Hail is another type of precipitation. It forms when ice crystals move up and down inside a cloud. Each time they rise, another layer of ice forms around them. Eventually, the hail becomes heavy enough to fall to the ground. Heavy hail can cause a lot of **damage**!

Go with the Flow

Sometimes rain freezes once it hits a surface, such as the road or a car. This is called freezing rain, or glaze. It can make the ground quite slippery!

Sometimes hail can fall even in the summer! Some hail chunks can be as large as baseballs.

It's Snowing!

When the temperature drops to 32 degrees Fahrenheit (0 degrees Celsius) or below, precipitation can fall as snow.

Tiny pieces of dirt or other matter float in the air. Ice crystals form around them and grow into snowflakes. A snowflake can be made of up to 200 ice crystals! When snowflakes become heavy enough, they fall to the ground. Many melt when they hit the ground. But if the ground is cold enough, snow can start to pile up. If the temperature stays cold enough, snow can stick around for a while!

Go with the Flow

Some snowflakes are small and light, while others are big and fluffy. Some snow even falls as hard, small balls called graupel.

You may have heard that no two snowflakes are exactly the same, but that's not true. In 1988, a scientist found two identical snow crystals.

It's a Blizzard out There

If a lot of snow falls in a short amount of time, it can cause big problems. Small flakes can soon pile up into feet of snow. Streets can be covered, making it hard to drive. People can be trapped in their homes. Snow can weigh down power lines, causing them to snap. This leaves people without electricity.

Blizzards are dangerous snowstorms with high winds. The winds often create large drifts of snow that can cover cars and, in extreme cases, even reach the tops of houses!

Go with the Flow

Lake-effect snowstorms and nor'easters are big storms that happen as wind moves over lakes and oceans. This causes water to evaporate and form big clouds that can drop a lot of precipitation.

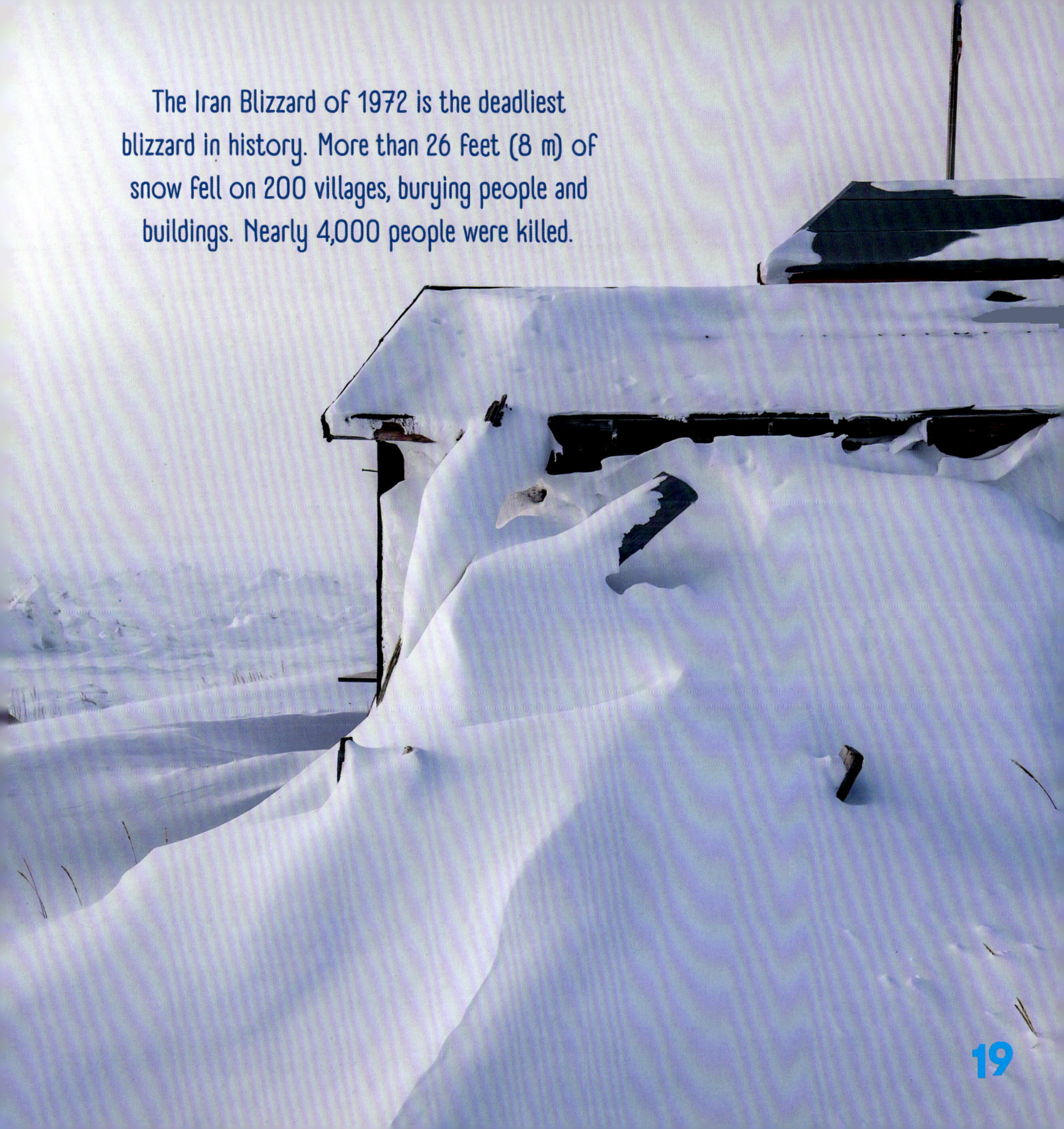

The Iran Blizzard of 1972 is the deadliest blizzard in history. More than 26 feet (8 m) of snow fell on 200 villages, burying people and buildings. Nearly 4,000 people were killed.

Climate Change

Extreme weather can be dangerous and even deadly. Scientists think the amount and **intensity** of precipitation will change, and possibly worsen, as **global climate change** continues.

Global climate change may cause big weather events, such as hurricanes and blizzards, to happen more often. It can also cause droughts, making it harder to live in areas that are too dry. We need water to survive, but too much or too little water can be dangerous. That's why it's important to take care of our planet!

Go with the Flow

Scientists think climate change is mostly caused by human activities, such as burning **fossil fuels** and cutting down trees.

Deadly Weather

	Where	Number of Deaths
1888: Schoolhouse Blizzard	Minnesota	235
1900: Great Galveston Hurricane	Texas	as many as 8,000
1972: Blizzard of 1972	Iran	4,000
2005: Hurricane Katrina	southeastern U.S.	1,800
2017: Hurricane Maria	Puerto Rico	nearly 3,000

Glossary

atmosphere: the mixture of gases that surrounds a planet

damage: harm

extreme: very great

food chain: a line of living things, each of which uses the one before it for food

fossil fuel: matter formed over millions of years from plant and animal remains that's burned for power

global climate change: long-term change in Earth's weather, caused partly by human activities such as burning oil and natural gas

hurricane: a violent storm with heavy rain and high winds

intensity: amount of strength or force

monsoon: a seasonal change in wind direction resulting in a change in precipitation

temperate: mild weather that's not too hot or too cold

tropical: having to do with the warm parts of Earth near the equator

water cycle: the series of conditions through which water passes from vapor in the air to liquid or solid falling on Earth's surface and finally rising back into the air

Fact Check

1. Some places, like ________, are very humid.
   a. deserts
   b. rainforests
   c. monsoons

2. What happens when snow melts as it falls and then freezes again before reaching the ground?
   a. snow
   b. rain
   c. sleet

3. ________ are big storms that happen as wind moves over lakes and oceans.
   a. Blizzards
   b. Hurricanes
   c. Nor'easters

Answers: 1. b, 2. c, 3. c

On the Internet

Precipitation and the Water Cycle
www.usgs.gov/water-science-school/science/precipitation-and-water-cycle
Learn more about how raindrops form and which areas of the world get the most precipitation.

The Water Cycle
https://gpm.nasa.gov/education/water-cycle
Get an up-close look at the water cycle from NASA!

Publisher's note to educators and parents: Our editors have carefully reviewed these websites to ensure that they are suitable for students. Many websites change frequently, however, and we cannot guarantee that a site's future contents will continue to meet our high standards of quality and educational value. Be advised that students should be closely supervised whenever they access the Internet.

Index